Drupal Rules How-to

Discover the power of the Rules framework to turn
your Drupal 7 installation into an action-based,
interactive application

Robert Varkonyi

PUBLISHING

BIRMINGHAM - MUMBAI

Drupal Rules How-to

First published: November 2012

Production Reference: 1161112

Published by Packt Publishing Ltd.
Livery Place
35 Livery Street
Birmingham B3 2PB, UK.

ISBN 978-1-84951-998-4

www.packtpub.com

Credits

Author
Robert Varkonyi

Reviewers
Veturi JV Subramanyeswari
Liran Tal

Acquisition Editor
Mary Jasmine Nadar

Commissioning Editors
Yogesh Dalvi
Shreerang Deshpande
Maria D'souza
Meeta Rajani

Technical Editor
Jalasha D'costa

Project Coordinator
Priya Sharma

Proofreader
Lesley Harrison

Production Coordinator
Melwyn D'sa

Cover Work
Melwyn D'sa

Cover Image
Conidon Miranda

About the Author

Robert Varkonyi is a senior Drupal developer who was involved in successful Drupal projects across the globe, including US, UK, Spain, Portugal, Netherlands, Belgium, France, Germany, Sweden, and Hungary. He's been working with Drupal since 2007 and gained deep experiences in enterprise level Drupal development. He enjoys developing custom modules and is a true fan of clear code, structured work, and coding standards.

During his career, Robert has worked for clients such as, NBC Universal, ITV, Ericsson, iVillage, CMC Markets, and Avanti Communications.

I'd like to thank to my friend David Toth, who introduced me to Drupal development and my girlfriend Alexandra Ujvary who accepted the change of priorities in our life during the writing of this book.

About the Reviewers

Sree (a.k.a **Veturi JV Subramanyeswari**) is currently working as a Solution Architect at a well known software consulting MNC in India. Prior to joining this company, she served few Indian MNCs, many startups, and R&D sectors in various roles such as, programmer, tech lead, research assistant, Architect, and so on. She has around more than eight years of working experience in web technologies covering media and entertainment, publishing, healthcare, enterprise architecture, manufacturing, public sector, defense communication, gaming, and so on. She is also a well known speaker who delivers talks on Drupal, Open Source, PHP, Women in Technology, and other such topics.

She reviewed other tech books such as:

- DevOps
- Twitter Bootstrap
- Drupal 7 Multi Sites Configuration
- Building Powerful and Robust Websites with Drupal 6
- Drupal 6 Module development
- PHP Team Development
- Drupal-6-site-blueprints
- Drupal 6 Attachment Views
- Drupal E-Commerce with Ubercart 2.x
- Drupal 7: First Look
- Twitter bootstrap
- Drupal SEO
- and many more

I would like to thank my family and friends who supported me in completing my reviews on time with good quality.

Liran Tal is a leading software developer, expert Linux engineer, and an avid supporter of the open source movement. In 2007, he has redefined network RADIUS management by establishing *daloRADIUS*, a world-recognized and industry-leading open source project.

Liran currently works at HP, leading the development team on a Drupal based collaboration platform in HP's Live Network department.

At HPLN, Liran plays a key role in system architecture design, shaping the technology strategy from planning and development to deployment, and maintenance in HP's IaaS cloud. Acting as the technological focal point, he loves mentoring his team mates, drive for better code methodology, and seek out innovative solutions to support business strategies.

He graduated cum laude in his Bachelor of Business and Information Systems Analysis studies and enjoys spending his time playing the guitar, hacking all things based on Linux, and continuously experimenting with and contributing to open source projects.

www.PacktPub.com

Support files, eBooks, discount offers and more

You might want to visit www.PacktPub.com for support files and downloads related to your book.

Did you know that Packt offers eBook versions of every book published, with PDF and ePub files available? You can upgrade to the eBook version at www.PacktPub.com and as a print book customer, you are entitled to a discount on the eBook copy. Get in touch with us at service@ packtpub.com for more details.

At www.PacktPub.com, you can also read a collection of free technical articles, sign up for a range of free newsletters and receive exclusive discounts and offers on Packt books and eBooks.

http://PacktLib.PacktPub.com

Do you need instant solutions to your IT questions? PacktLib is Packt's online digital book library. Here, you can access, read and search across Packt's entire library of books.

Why Subscribe?

- ► Fully searchable across every book published by Packt
- ► Copy and paste, print and bookmark content
- ► On demand and accessible via web browser

Free Access for Packt account holders

If you have an account with Packt at www.PacktPub.com, you can use this to access PacktLib today and view nine entirely free books. Simply use your login credentials for immediate access.

Table of Contents

Preface

This book will demonstrate the power of the Rules framework that enables you to turn your Drupal 7 installation into an event- and action-based, interactive application. Drupal Rules How-to is a practical, hands-on guide that provides you with a number of clear step-by-step exercises, which will help you take advantage of the real power of the Rules framework, and understand how to use it on a site builder and developer level.

What this book covers

Understanding the basics of Reaction Rules (Must Know), demonstrates the basic use of Reaction Rules by creating a simple rule configuration and explaining how Events, Conditions, and Actions work.

Displaying a message on the site (Must Know), describes the steps to be taken in order to display a custom message on the site after creating a new article.

Sending e-mail notifications (Must Know), explains how to send a customized e-mail notification to all administrators when a new user registers on the website.

Sending notifications if someone comments on a node created by another user (Must Know), explains how to send a new comment notification e-mail to a node author using replacement patterns.

Using loops and lists (Must Know), demonstrates the basics of loops and lists by creating a list of objects in Rules and executing an Action on each item.

Components – Reusing Rules, Conditions, and Actions (Must Know), explains the benefits of using Rules components by creating a Condition that can be re-used in other rule configurations.

Using the Rules Scheduler (Must Know), demonstrates the Rules Scheduler by creating a rule configuration that sends a reminder e-mail to all users who haven't signed in for a week.

Debugging Rules (Must Know), explains how to use the built-in Rules Debug feature and provides hints and best practices.

Using PHP in Conditions and Actions (Should Know), demonstrates how to use PHP input in Conditions and Actions and provides hints regarding security and usage.

Using condition groups (Should Know), describes the usage of Condition groups and the ability to combine Conditions by creating a rule configuration that sends an e-mail to the administrators if either a new article or any content type gets posted on the site that has an image field

Subscribe to comments on a node using Rules and Flag (Should Know), explains how to use Rules and Flag to send out e-mail notifications to users when someone comments on a node users are subscribed to.

Adding a Taxonomy term to a node using Views Bulk Operations and Rules (Should Know), demonstrates how to execute Rules components on a Views Bulk Operations (VBO) view and explains how to expose components for VBO to work with.

Loading a list of objects into Rules using VBO (Should Know), describes how to add a specific taxonomy term to a list of nodes using Views Bulk Operations (VBO) and Rules.

Rules Bonus Pack (Should Know), demonstrates the Rules Bonus Pack module, which is a set of extensions and integrations with other modules to extend Rules to provide additional Events, Conditions and Actions, and also integrate with other modules, such as CTools.

Providing new Events, Conditions and Actions (Become an Expert), explains how to create custom Events, Conditions, and Actions for Rules by providing an example scenario where the number of times a view gets rendered is tracked by Rules.

Providing new entity tokens (Become an Expert), explains the basics of entity tokens and demonstrates how to create a new one that can be used in rule configurations.

Executing Rules programmatically (Become an Expert), explains how to execute Actions, Rules or rule sets programmatically by creating a new rule configuration and executing it from code.

Providing new variables for Actions (Become an Expert), explains how to modify existing or provide new variables and data for Rules in Actions by extending a previously defined Action that provides additional data to Rules after the Action is executed

Providing default rule configurations (Become an Expert), explains how to provide default rule configurations in code so that configurations can be maintained in code and version control, such as SVN or Git.

What you need for this book

A fully functional Drupal 7 installation is needed in order to complete the exercises in this book. Also, the following modules need to be installed and enabled:

- Rules
- Rules UI
- Rules Scheduler
- Views
- Flag
- Views Bulk Operations
- Rules Bonus Pack

While the exercises in this book are written in a manner that aims to clearly and deeply explain each step, they presume that the reader has got basic understanding of the Drupal user interface.

Who this book is for

This book is for Drupal site builders and developers who want to take full advantage of the Rules framework's power and flexibility.

Conventions

In this book, you will find a number of styles of text that distinguish between different kinds of information. Here are some examples of these styles, and an explanation of their meaning.

Code words in text are shown as follows: "It is also possible to modify a default rule configuration in code. For that we could use `hook_default_rules_configuration_alter()` in our `*.rules_defaults.inc` file."

A block of code is set as follows:

```
/**
 * Implements hook_rules_event_info()
 * Define our new custom event for Rules
 */
function custom_rules_event_info() {
  return array(
    'custom_views_render' =>  array (
      'label' => 'A view is rendered',
      'group' => 'Rules Custom',
      'variables' => array(
        'view' => array(
```

```
                'type' => 'custom_view_datatype',
                'label' => t('View being rendered')
            )
        )
    )
    );
}
```

New terms and **important words** are shown in bold. Words that you see on the screen, in menus or dialog boxes for example, appear in the text like this: " In the **MESSAGE** field, we've used **REPLACEMENT PATTERNS** to insert chunks of data from the objects available in our current rule configuration.".

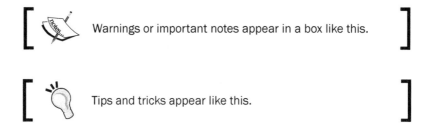

Warnings or important notes appear in a box like this.

Tips and tricks appear like this.

Reader feedback

Feedback from our readers is always welcome. Let us know what you think about this book—what you liked or may have disliked. Reader feedback is important for us to develop titles that you really get the most out of.

To send us general feedback, simply send an e-mail to feedback@packtpub.com, and mention the book title via the subject of your message.

If there is a book that you need and would like to see us publish, please send us a note in the **SUGGEST A TITLE** form on www.packtpub.com or e-mail suggest@packtpub.com.

If there is a topic that you have expertise in and you are interested in either writing or contributing to a book, see our author guide on www.packtpub.com/authors.

Customer support

Now that you are the proud owner of a Packt book, we have a number of things to help you to get the most from your purchase.

Errata

Although we have taken every care to ensure the accuracy of our content, mistakes do happen. If you find a mistake in one of our books—maybe a mistake in the text or the code—we would be grateful if you would report this to us. By doing so, you can save other readers from frustration and help us improve subsequent versions of this book. If you find any errata, please report them by visiting http://www.packtpub.com/support, selecting your book, clicking on the **errata submission form** link, and entering the details of your errata. Once your errata are verified, your submission will be accepted and the errata will be uploaded on our website, or added to any list of existing errata, under the Errata section of that title. Any existing errata can be viewed by selecting your title from http://www.packtpub.com/support.

Piracy

Piracy of copyright material on the Internet is an ongoing problem across all media. At Packt, we take the protection of our copyright and licenses very seriously. If you come across any illegal copies of our works, in any form, on the Internet, please provide us with the location address or website name immediately so that we can pursue a remedy.

Please contact us at copyright@packtpub.com with a link to the suspected pirated material.

We appreciate your help in protecting our authors, and our ability to bring you valuable content.

Questions

You can contact us at questions@packtpub.com if you are having a problem with any aspect of the book, and we will do our best to address it

Drupal Rules How-to

Welcome to Drupal Rules. This book aims to present site builders and developers with tutorials that help them leverage the power of the Rules framework and turn their Drupal sites into event – action-based, interactive applications.

Rules can be used for building complex and flexible systems that respond to various system events, such as node creation, user registration, or viewing a comment. This book demonstrates the Rules framework in a learning curve style: from the basics, such as Reaction Rules, Events, Conditions, Actions, Components, and Scheduler, through advanced features such as using PHP in Conditions and Actions, combining Rules with other modules such as Views Bulk Operations and Flag to further extend the flexibility, to expertise API examples such as providing custom Events, Conditions, and Actions, creating new entity tokens and default rule configurations, and executing rule configurations programmatically.

Understanding the basics of Reaction Rules (Must know)

This section describes the basics of Reaction Rules, Events, Conditions, and Actions.

We'll create a simple rule that makes newly created articles sticky.

Getting ready

Enable the **Rules** and **Rules UI** modules on your site.

How to do it...

1. Go to **Configuration | Workflow | Rules**.

2. Click on **Add new rule**.

3. Enter a name for this rule configuration, as shown in the following screenshot:

4. Enter values for **Tags** if required (they can be useful for categorizing rule configurations).

5. Set the Event to **Node**, after saving new content.

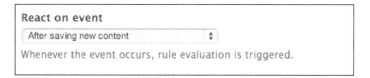

6. Go to the Condition, **Node | Content is of type** and set the value to **Article** by selecting it in the select box.

7. Add an Action, **Data** | **Data selector** and select the sticky field of the node.

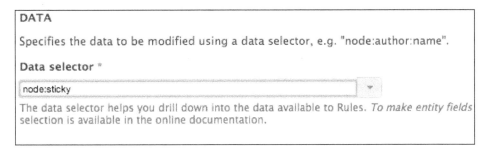

DATA

Specifies the data to be modified using a data selector, e.g. "node:author:name".

Data selector *

node:sticky

The data selector helps you drill down into the data available to Rules. *To make entity fields* selection is available in the online documentation.

8. Hit **Continue**.
9. Tick the **Value** checkbox.

VALUE

The new value to set for the specified data.
☑ Value

Switch to data selection

10. Click on **Save**.

How it works...

With the following steps, we're telling Rules to do the following: whenever a new content has been created and its content type is **Article**, set its **sticky** value to TRUE. This rule configuration will be executed every time a new article has been created.

There's more

Let's have a look at the way Events, Conditions, and Actions work.

Events

A reaction rule always needs a specified event to happen on the site so it will execute. This can be done when a user logs in, when a node is created, or various other Events are provided by Rules (or other contributed/custom modules). Events may provide variables that can be used in the configuration. For example, if the event is **Node** | **After saving new content**, the created content object will be available in the rest of the rule configurations for Rules to work with.

A reaction rule can have multiple triggering Events. For example, we can execute the same Action when we delete a node or when we delete a comment.

Conditions

We can use Conditions to check some data, that's available in our current configuration, because we usually want to execute an Action only if certain criteria are matching. For example, we might want to check a node's type (**Content is of type**), whether a node has a particular field (**Entity has field**) or a truth value (**Data comparison**). There are a number of Conditions provided by default, but it's also possible to create our own Conditions in our custom module.

Conditions can be grouped into AND or OR groups. These groups can be used to create complex Conditions and each group may have additional AND and OR groups.

Actions

Rules Actions are tasks that Rules may perform. There are a number of Actions that Rules provides by default, such as setting a value, publishing a node, or creating a new entity. Other than the core Actions, we can also create Actions in a custom module.

Displaying a message on the site (Must know)

This recipe describes the steps to be taken in order to display a custom message on the site after creating a new article.

Getting ready

All recipes in this book assume that the reader is familiar with the Rules UI and/or has read the first recipe in this book, *Understanding the basics of Reaction Rules (Must know)*.

How to do it...

1. Create a new rule configuration and set the event to **Node | After saving new content**.

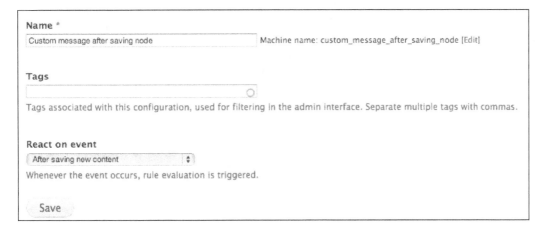

2. Add a condition, **Node | Content is of type** and set **CONTENT TYPES** to **Article**, as shown in the following screenshot:

3. Add an Action and select **System | Show a message on the site**.

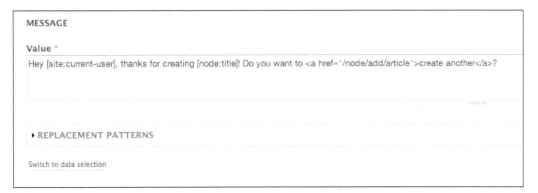

How it works...

By using the Action, **After saving new content**, we're asking Rules to react on content creation. This means that the rule will fire every time a new content has been created in the system. By using Conditions, we can tell Rules to only fire the action if the created content type is **Article** (or any other content type). In the **MESSAGE** field, we've used **REPLACEMENT PATTERNS** to insert chunks of data from the objects available in our current rule configuration.

Sending e-mail notifications (Must know)

This recipe explains how to send a customized e-mail notification to administrators when a new user registers on the website.

How to do it...

1. Create a new rule configuration and set the event to **User | After saving new user account**.

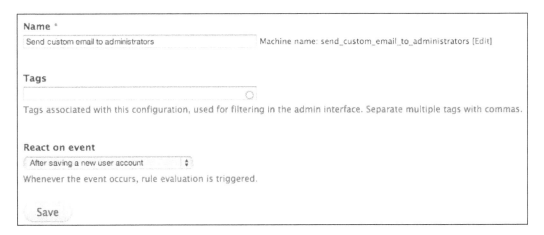

2. Add an action **System | Send mail to all users of a role**.
3. Select the role you want the e-mails to be sent to.

4. Enter the subject of the mail in the **Value** section under **SUBJECT**.

SUBJECT

The mail's subject.

Value *

New user account

---

5. Enter the body of the e-mail in the **MESSAGE | Value** section.

MESSAGE

The mail's message body.

Value *

Hey Administrator!

[account:name] has created a new account at [account:created]

[site:name]

How it works...

In this rule configuration, we're telling Rules to act on new user registrations and send e-mail notifications to the site administrators when this event occurs. In the e-mail body we've used **REPLACEMENT PATTERNS** to display the new user's username, the date and time the account was created, and the site's name will be used as the signature.

There's more...

While this example is very useful and easy to configure, site builders are advised to use it with care. It is not advised to use this action to send e-mails to a large number of users. Because every action is executed right after an event occurred, it can put a serious load on the server(s) and can cause the site to go down.

Sending notifications if someone comments on a node created by another user (Must know)

If we want to send e-mails to individual users, it's better to use the **Send mail** Action in our rule configuration. A good use case could be when we want to notify a node's author when someone leaves a comment on a node created by them. We could then use the Event **Comment | After saving a new comment**, then add two Actions.

How to do it...

The following steps will help you send notifications if a user comments on a node created by another user:

1. In the first Action, we need to load the author of the node that's being commented on. For that we can use **Data | Add a variable** Action and set the value of **TYPE** to **User**:

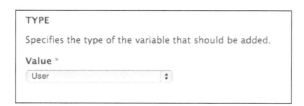

2. We then set the value to the node's author.

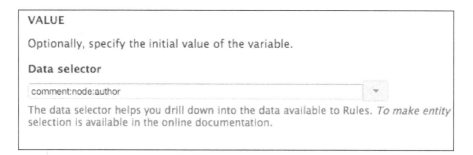

3. Optionally, we can set the label of the variable, so we can easily identify it in the next step:

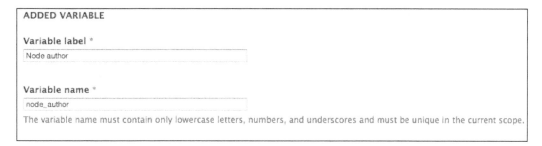

4. We add another Action, **System | Send mail** and use **REPLACEMENT PATTERNS** to make use of the variable we added in the previous step.

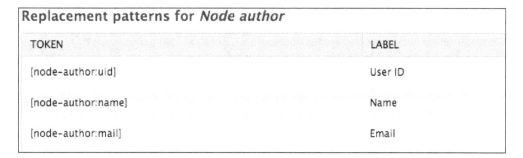

5. We can then use **node-author:mail** in the **To** field which is the e-mail address of the original node author.

6. If we don't want the author to be notified of their own comments, we can add a Condition, **Data | Data comparison** and set the **DATA TO COMPARE** value to the user ID of the node author, as shown in the following screenshot:

7. Next, we hit **Continue** and set the data value to the user ID of the comment author, as shown in the following screenshot:

DATA VALUE

The value to compare the data with.

Data selector *

comment:author:uid

The data selector helps you drill down into the data available to Rules. *To make entity fields appear* selection is available in the online documentation.

8. This configuration is of course incorrect at this stage, as Rules would only send an e-mail if the **Node** author and the **Comment** author are the same, which is the opposite of what we're looking for. A really good feature in Rules is **Negate**. This setting basically sets **TRUE** values to **FALSE** and vice versa, which is just what we currently need. The Negate feature is shown in the following screenshot:

☑ Negate

    If checked, the condition result is negated such that it returns TRUE if it evaluates to FALSE.

This way the rule will only fire if the author of **Node** is not the same as the author of **Comment**.

There's more...

The following section will throw light on how to send notifications only to users wanting to receive them.

Sending notifications only if the user wants to receive them

For usability or to avoid our site users from feeling spammed, ideally we would want to add a new Boolean checkbox field to the user object that is used as a switch to indicate whether the user wants to receive these notifications from our site or not. Then in our rule configuration, we can use the Condition, **Data | Data value is empty** and set the **Data selector** value to that field. Assuming that the name of the field is **field-notifications**, it would look like the following screenshot:

DATA TO CHECK

The data to be checked to be empty, specified by using a data selector, e.g. "node:author:name".

Data selector *

comment:node:author:field-notifications|

The data selector helps you drill down into the data available to Rules. *To make entity fields appear in the data* selection is available in the online documentation.

This configuration is of course incorrect at this stage, as Rules would only send an e-mail if the field is empty (the user does *not* want notifications), which is the opposite of what we're looking for. So we need to use **Negate.**

This way the rule will only fire if that particular user has checked the **Notifications** field on his/her user account page.

Using loops and lists (Must know)

This recipe explains the basics of lists and loops, creating a list of objects, and executing an action on each item.

How to do it...

1. Create a new rule configuration and set the Event to **Node | After saving new content**.

2. Add a Condition, **Node | Content is of type** and set it to **Article**.

3. Add a new loop and set **Data selector** to **node:field-tags**.

4. Add a new Action **System | Show a message on the site** and set a message.

MESSAGE

Value *

"[list-item:name]" has been added to [node:title]

How it works...

Using lists and loops in Rules is the way to handle multiple value fields and execute Actions on each individual item. While this particular recipe is not too useful in the real world, it can be used as a basis for more advanced features, for example, when using a node reference field to provide reference to a list of related nodes. We can then load that list of referenced nodes and create a loop that will send a customized e-mail notification to the authors of the referenced nodes.

There's more...

We can also add items to a list by adding an Action, **Data | Add an item to a list**. An example use case could be to automatically add a taxonomy term to the newly created node or add a user to a user reference list.

Components – Reusing Rules, Conditions, and Actions (Must know)

This recipe explains the benefits of using Components by creating a Condition that can be re-used in other rule configurations.

In this scenario, we want to perform some action when a node is being commented on. But we only want to execute the action if the node was *not* created by the super admin (that is, user 1) *and* the node is either an article, or has an image field (`field_image`).

How to do it...

1. Go to **Configuration | Workflow | Rules | Components**.
2. Add a new component and set the plugin to **Condition set (AND)**.
3. Enter a name for the component and add a parameter **Entity | Node**.

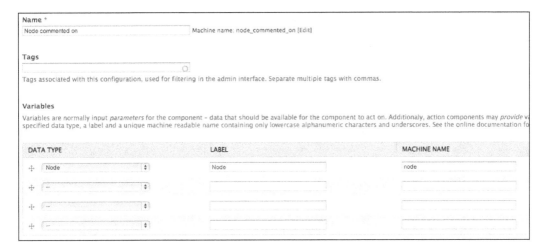

4. Add a Condition, **Data comparison**, set the value to the author of the node, set **OPERATOR** to **equals**, enter **1** in the **Data value** field and tick **Negate**.

5. Add an OR group by clicking on **Add or**, as shown in the following screenshot:

6. Add a Condition, **Node | Content is of type** and set it to **Article**.

7. Add a Condition, **Entity | Entity has field**, set **Entity** to **node**, and select the field, **field_image**, as shown in the following screenshot:

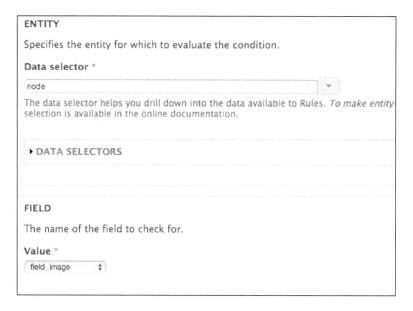

ENTITY

Specifies the entity for which to evaluate the condition.

Data selector *

node

The data selector helps you drill down into the data available to Rules. *To make entity* selection is available in the online documentation.

▸ DATA SELECTORS

FIELD

The name of the field to check for.

Value *

field_image

8. Organize the Conditions so that the last two Conditions are in the OR group we created before.

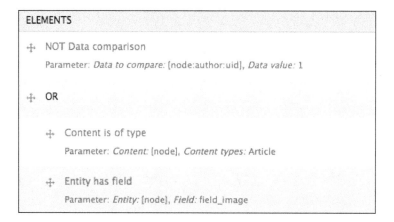

ELEMENTS

⊹ NOT Data comparison
   Parameter: *Data to compare:* [node:author:uid], *Data value:* 1

⊹ OR

   ⊹ Content is of type
      Parameter: *Content:* [node], *Content types:* Article

   ⊹ Entity has field
      Parameter: *Entity:* [node], *Field:* field_image

9. Create a new rule configuration and set the Event to **Comment | After saving a new comment**.

10. Add a new Condition and select the component that we created. An example is shown in the following screenshot:

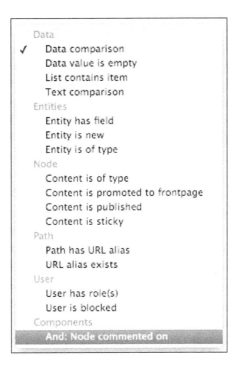

11. Select **comment:node** as the parameter.

12. Add a new Action, **System | Show a message on the site** and configure the message.

How it works...

Components require parameters to be specified, that will be used as placeholders for the objects we want to execute a rule configuration on. Depending on what our goal is, we can select from the core Rules data types, entities, or lists.

In this example, we've added a **Node** parameter to the component, because we wanted to see who is the node's author, if it's an article or if it has an image field. Then in our Condition, we've provided the actual object on which we've evaluated the Condition. If you're familiar with programming, then you'll see that components are just like functions; they expect parameters and can be re-used in other scenarios.

There's more...

The main benefit of using Rules components is that we can re-use complex Conditions, Actions, and other rule configurations. That means that we don't have to configure the same settings over and over again. Instead we can create components and use them in our rule configurations.

Other benefits also include exportability: components can be exported individually, which is a very useful addition when using configuration management, such as **Features**.

Components can also be executed on the UI, which is very useful for debugging and can also save a lot of development time.

Other component types

Apart from Condition sets, there are a few other component types we can use. They are as follows:

- ▶ **Action set**

  As the name suggests, this is a set of Actions, executed one after the other. It can be useful when we have a certain chain of Actions that we want to execute in various scenarios.

- ▶ **Rule**

  We can also create a rule configuration as a component to be used in other rule configurations. Think about a scenario when you want to perform an action on a list of node references (which would require a looped Action) but only if those nodes were created before 2012. While it is not possible to create a Condition within an Action, we can create a `Rule` component so we can add a Condition and an Action within the component itself and then use it as the Action of the other rule configuration.

▶ **Rule set**

Rule sets are a set of Rules, executed one after the other. It can be useful when we want to execute a chain of Rules when an event occurs.

Parameters and provided variables

Condition sets require parameters which are **input data** for the component. These are the variables that need to be specified so that the Condition can evaluate to FALSE or TRUE.

Action sets, Rules, and Rule sets can *provide* variables. That means they can *return* data after the action is executed.

Using the Rules Scheduler (Must know)

In this recipe we create a rule configuration that sends a reminder e-mail to a user that hasn't logged in to the website for a week.

Getting ready

We need to make sure that the **Rules Scheduler** module is enabled.

How to do it...

1. Create a new Action set component and provide a user object as a parameter.

2. Add a new Action, **System | Send mail** and configure the various fields, set the **To** field to **[user:mail]**, enter a subject and fill in the **MESSAGE** field with something such as Hey, you haven't logged in to our site for a week now....

3. Add a new rule configuration and set the Event to **User | User has logged in**.

4. Add an Action, **Rules scheduler | Schedule component evaluation**.

5. Select the component which we created in step 1.

6. Click on **Switch to direct input mode** and enter **+7 days**.

SCHEDULED EVALUATION DATE

Value *

+7 days

The date in GMT. You may enter a fixed time (like *2012-06-18 12:53:37*)

Switch to data selection

---

7. Set a unique identifier to this scheduled component.

> IDENTIFIER
>
> A string used for identifying this task. Any existing tasks for this component
>
> Value
>
> Send login reminder to [account:uid]

8. Provide the **account** object to the component.

How it works...

In this example we wanted to send reminder e-mails to individual users, who haven't logged in to the website for a week. For that we've created a component (that executes the **Send mail** Action), which we use in our rule configuration as a scheduled component. In the rule configuration, we set the Event to **User has logged in** because we want to set the scheduled date to a week from the user's last login. Please note that you'll need **cron** running for the scheduler to work.

There's more...

Additionally, we would probably want to add an Action **Delete scheduled tasks**, using the same identifier we've used for the scheduled component and place it before the **Schedule component evaluation** Action.

> Actions
>
> ELEMENTS
>
> ╬ Delete scheduled tasks
>   Parameter: *Component:* Send login reminder, *Task identifier:* Send login reminder to ...
>
> ╬ Schedule component evaluation
>   Parameter: *Component:* Send login reminder, *Scheduled evaluation date:* +7 days, *Identifier:* Send login reminder to ..., *User:* [account]

This way we make sure that the scheduled date always gets updated when the user logs in and new reminders get scheduled.

Schedule UI

`Rules Scheduler` provides a user interface through the `Views` module which can be found at **Configuration | Workflow | Rules | Schedule**. This interface can be very useful as it displays all the components that are scheduled for execution. It is also a very useful tool for debugging scheduled components.

Debugging Rules (Must know)

This recipe explains how to debug the rule configurations using the user interface.

How to do it...

1. Go to **Configuration | Workflow | Rules | Settings**.
2. Set **Show debug information** to **Always**.
3. Save the form.

DEBUGGING

☐ Log debug information to the system log

Show debug information

○ Never

○ In case of errors

◉ Always

Debug information is only shown when rules are evaluated and is visible for users having the

Default theme region

| Help ⬍ |

The region, where the debug log should be displayed on the default theme *bartik*. For other t

Admin theme region

| Help ⬍ |

The region, where the debug log should be displayed on the admin theme *seven*.

How it works

Rules provides a very useful debugging system. This allows us to follow all the steps of a rule configuration as it's being executed. The following screenshot will show you if the Conditions evaluate and how long each step takes:

```
▼ Rules evaluation log
  ▼ "Reacting on event After saving new content.
  • 0 ms Reacting on event After saving new content.
  • 7.268 ms Evaluating conditions of rule Make new Articles sticky. [edit]
  • 7.587 ms The condition node_is_of_type evaluated to TRUE [edit]
  • 7.603 ms AND evaluated to TRUE.
  •  ▼ "Rule Make new Articles sticky fires. [edit]
      ○ 0 ms Rule Make new Articles sticky fires.
      ○ 1.325 ms Evaluating the action data_set. [edit]
      ○ 1.434 ms Rule Make new Articles sticky has fired.
  • 9.08 ms Saved node of type node.
  • 16.348 ms Finished reacting on event After saving new content.
```

This is useful when our rule configuration doesn't work the way we want it to. It's always advised to use the debugger to see if the Conditions we used to evaluate the way we want them to. It's also useful that we're able to see how long each step takes. In this case, 16 ms is not a huge overhead when creating a node. However, if our rule configuration is set to fire Actions on each page load, it might lead to problems and it's advised to refactor that particular configuration.

There's more...

Despite there being user permissions related to the display of debugging information, it's advised that on production sites we don't display debug information on the UI. Instead, we make Rules write the logs into the log file by setting the value **Log debug information to the system log** on the **Settings** page, as shown in the following screenshot:

```
DEBUGGING
☑ Log debug information to the system log
```

The following recipes describe some more advanced features of the Rules framework, including the usage of PHP in Conditions and Actions and explains how to use Rules together with other modules, such as Flag, Views Bulk Operations, and Rules Bonus Pack.

Using PHP in Conditions and Actions (Should know)

This section explains how to use PHP input in Conditions and Actions.

In this simple example we'll display a message on the front page every Monday. To do that, we'll use a PHP input in our Condition to evaluate to TRUE if we're currently on the front page of our site, and if it's Monday today.

Getting ready

Enable the PHP Filter module on Drupal's module list page and assign relevant permissions if necessary. Take extra care as to whom you assign these permissions to, as the PHP input may cause security concerns so you probably don't want everyone on your website to be able to use it.

How to do it...

1. Add a new rule configuration and set the Event to **System | Drupal is initializing**.

2. Add a new Condition, **Data | Data comparison** and set it to **site:current-date**.

3. In the **DATA VALUE** field set, click on **Switch to data selection** and enter site:current-date.

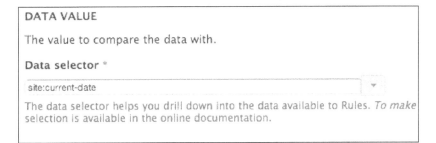

4. In the **PHP EVALUATION** field, enter the **Code** value, as shown in the following screenshot, and save the Condition:

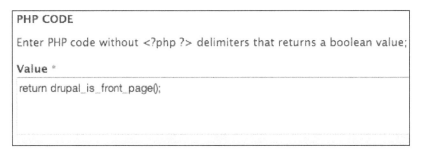

```
▼ PHP EVALUATION

Enter PHP code to process the selected argument value.

Code
return format_date($value, 'custom', 'D') == 'Mon';




Enter PHP code without <?php ?> delimiters that returns the processed
```

5. Add a new Condition and set the handler to **PHP | Execute custom PHP code** and enter this code in the text area:

```
PHP CODE

Enter PHP code without <?php ?> delimiters that returns a boolean value;

Value *
return drupal_is_front_page();


```

6. Add a new Action, **System | Show a message on the site** and enter the following **Value**, as shown in the screenshot:

```
Value *
Hey, have a good Monday!


```

How it works...

In the first Condition, we compare the current date value to figure out what day it is today. In the **PHP Evaluation** field, we always receive the value of the selected field in the `$value` variable, which in this case is a timestamp of the current date. We're using this value in Drupal's `format_date()` function to return TRUE if it's Monday today.

In the second Condition, we're returning TRUE if the current page we're visiting is the front page of our website.

There's more...

PHP can be put to use in many other ways too. Some are described as follows:

Using PHP in Actions

We can also use PHP in Actions to execute functions, update database entries, and perform other tasks as required. To do that we can add an Action, **Execute custom PHP code**, and enter the PHP code we want to execute.

Best practice

Using a PHP input in Rules is a very effective way to create custom Conditions and Actions if we don't want to programmatically create new ones in our custom module (more on that in the *Providing new Events, Conditions, and Actions (Become an expert)* recipe in this book). However, there are a number of things we want to keep in mind:

▶ **Permissions**

It is highly advised that we don't let regular users use the **PHP input filter**, as it is a high security risk.

▶ **Never use delimiters**

We should never use the `<?php ?>` delimiters in our custom code. Rules takes care of that for us. If we use the delimiters in our Condition or Action, it won't work.

▶ **Always test on a development site**

Of course, it is advised that all Rules configurations are tested on a development site before using them on production sites. This is particularly valid for configurations that include the PHP code in Conditions or Actions. We always want to make sure we enter code without typos, execute the right database commands, or update the right user information.

It is also advised that **Debugging** is turned on on our development site, that way we can save a lot of time testing our configuration.

Using condition groups (Should know)

This recipe describes the usage of condition groups and the ability to combine Conditions.

We'll create a rule that sends an e-mail to the administrators if either a new article or any content type gets posted on the site that has an image field (`field_image`).

How to do it...

1. Create a new rule configuration and set the Event to **Node | After saving new content**.

2. Add a new Condition, **Entities | Entity is new**.

3. Add an OR Group.

> **+** Add condition   **+** Add or   **+** Add and

4. Add a new Condition to the group by clicking on **Add condition** in the group's row, as shown in the following screenshot:

> edit   delete   Add condition   Add or   Add and

5. Add the Condition, **Node | Content is of type** and set the content type to **Article**.

6. Add another Condition to the OR group, use **Entities | Entity has field** and set the field to `field_image`.

7. Add an Action to the rule configuration, use **System | Send email to all users of a role**, select the **administrators** role and fill out the **SUBJECT** and **MESSAGE** fields.

How it works...

To create complex Conditions, in Rules we can use condition groups. This way we can create a chain of Conditions using AND or OR groups. **AND** groups require all Conditions within the group to evaluate to TRUE, while **OR** groups require only one Condition to evaluate to TRUE.

There's more...

The following section describes combining of conditional groups:

Combining condition groups

We can also combine condition groups, that means we can create condition groups within condition groups. Again, it is advised that **Debugging** is turned on when creating nested condition groups as it can save a lot of time figuring out why a configuration doesn't work as expected.

Subscribe to comments on a node using Rules and Flag (Should know)

This recipe explains how to use Rules and Flag to send out e-mail notifications to users when someone comments on a node users are subscribed to.

Getting ready

Install and enable the `Flag` module.

How to do it...

1. Create a new flag configuration at **Structure | Flags**.

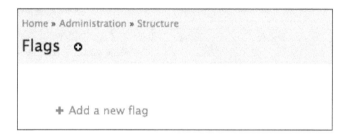

2. Enter a name and set the type to **Nodes**.

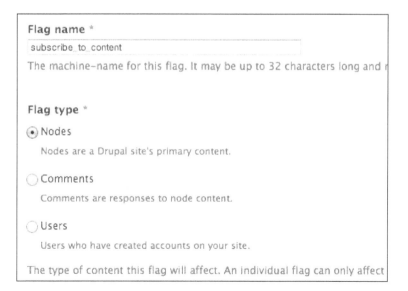

3. Enter `Subscribe` as the label for the new Flag and set and **Flaggable content** to **Article**, as shown in the following screenshot, and save the Flag configuration:

4. Create a new rule configuration at **Configuration | Workflow | Rules**, set the Event to **Comment | After saving a new comment**.

5. Add an Action, **Flag | Fetch users who have flagged a node**, as shown in the following screenshot:

6. Set the Flag to the new flag configuration we created.

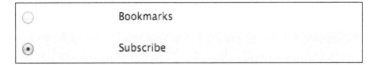

7. We want to act on the node the comment belongs to, so we'll use the comment's node in the **Data selector** field and save the Action, as shown in the following screenshot:

8. Add a new loop in the **Actions** section and select **users** in the **Data selector** section, as shown in the following screenshot:

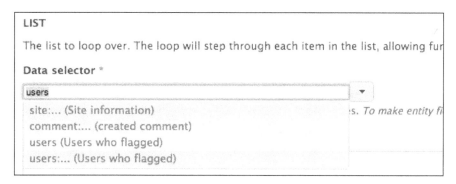

9. Optionally, set the variable name to something that's more descriptive, as shown in the following screenshot, and save the loop.

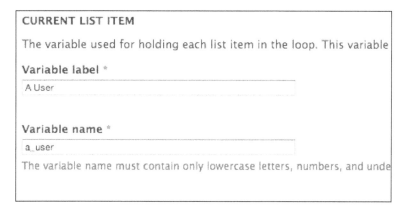

10. Add a new Action within the loop **System | Send mail** and configure the various fields using **REPLACEMENT PATTERNS**.

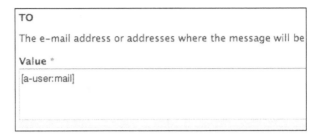

11. Fill in the **TO** text area. Note, that we make use of **a-user:mail** token, which became available to Rules in the previous step, when defining the loop and setting the labels of the current list item.

12. Enter the subject. Again, the **a-user:name** token is used, which will be replaced with the name of the user in the loop.

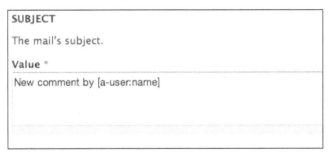

13. Enter the message. Here we make use of other available tokens. This is shown in the following screenshot:

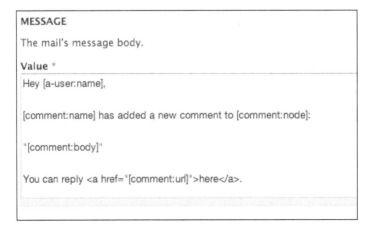

How it works...

In this recipe, we're creating a new flag configuration for article nodes and using that in our rule configuration to get the list of users that are subscribed to a node that's being commented on (using the Flag we created), and send them a notification e-mail. Flag provides a list data type (**Fetch users who have flagged a node**) that Rules can use to create a loop of all users who flagged a node, and act on each individual object.

There's more...

Flag provides various Events, Conditions, and Actions that we can use in our rule configurations.

Events

A node can be flagged or unflagged: This acts on Events that involve flagging or unflagging a node, user, or comment.

Conditions

The following are the Conditions provided by Flag:

Node/Comment/User is flagged: This checks if the entity is already flagged.

Node/Comment/User has flagging count: This checks the number of flags an entity has.

Actions

The Action for fetch users who have flagged a comment/node/user creates a list of users who have flagged an entity. The data will be provided to Rules as a list type, so it can execute a looped action on each individual object.

Flag a comment/node/user: This programmatically flags an entity.

Trim a flag: This sets the maximum number of flags an entity can have.

Unflag a comment/node/user: This programmatically unflags an entity.

Adding a taxonomy term to a node using Views Bulk Operations and Rules (Should know)

This recipe describes how to add a specific taxonomy term to a list of nodes using **Views Bulk Operations** (**VBO**) and Rules.

Getting ready

Install and enable Views, Views UI, and Views Bulk Operations. Go to **Structure | Views** and create a new table view that lists all nodes posted on the site, and add a **Bulk operations: Content** field to it.

How to do it...

1. Create a new rule component, select the **Rule** plugin and require an **Entity | Node** parameter. Name the new component Add taxonomy term to node.

2. Add a Condition, **Entities | Entity has field**, use node as the entity, and set the field to **field_tags**.

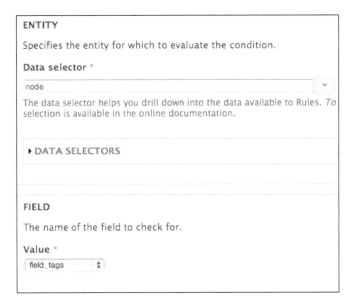

3. Add a new Action, **Data | Add an item to a list** and set the value to **node:field-tags**.

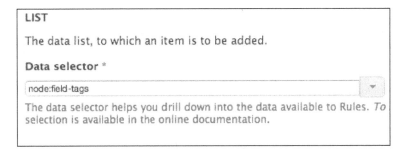

4. In the **Item to add** fieldset, click on the **Switch to the direct input mode** button and enter the ID of the taxonomy term to add, as shown in the following screenshot:

> ITEM TO ADD
>
> Taxonomy term identifier *
>
> | 1 |
>
> Specify an identifier of a taxonomy term.
>
> Switch to data selection

5. Go back to the view and click on the **Bulk Operations: Content** field.

6. In the popup window, select the rule component we created in the **SELECTED OPERATIONS** fieldset, as shown in the following screenshot:

> ▼ SELECTED OPERATIONS
>
> ☑ Add taxonomy term to node (rules_add_taxonomy_term_to_node)
>
>   ☐ Enqueue the operation instead of executing it directly
>
>   ☐ Skip confirmation step
>
>   ☐ Override label

How it works...

Views Bulk Operations can use Rules components to execute Actions on a list of entities and objects. We can create the Rules components with parameters and VBO will make these components available as operations in our Bulk Operations field configuration, if the field type matches the component's parameter type. For example, when creating a component that requires a `Node` parameter, we need to add the same type of VBO field (**Content: Bulk Operations**) to the view, because this is how VBO determines what kind of parameter is being passed to Rules.

There's more...

If we want this feature to be a bit more flexible and choose a taxonomy term, we want to add to the nodes instead of always adding a preconfigured term ID, we can do the following:

1. Add a new **Entity | Taxonomy** term parameter to our component, set the machine name to the term.

2. Edit our Action, **Add an item to a list**, in the **Item to add** fieldset, click on **Switch to data selection**, and enter **term**. This is given in the following screenshot:

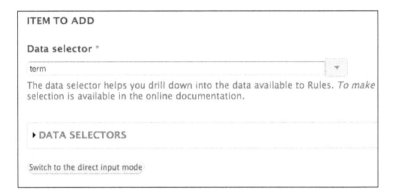

ITEM TO ADD

Data selector *

term

The data selector helps you drill down into the data available to Rules. *To make* selection is available in the online documentation.

▸ DATA SELECTORS

Switch to the direct input mode

Now when executing the operation, VBO will display a configuration screen where we can enter the ID of the taxonomy term we want to add to the node.

Loading a list of objects into Rules using VBO (Should know)

This recipe explains how to load the result of a VBO view into Rules.

We will create a view that lists all nodes that are:

▸ Created by user 1 (admin)

▸ Promoted to the front page

▸ More than two weeks old

We will then demote these nodes from the front page using Rules.

Getting ready

Install and enable Views, Views UI, and Views Bulk Operations.

How to do it...

1. Go to **Structure | Views** and create a new view that lists all the nodes that are created by user 1, are promoted to front page, and are more than two weeks old, and add a VBO field to it. Call this new view **Old admin content**.

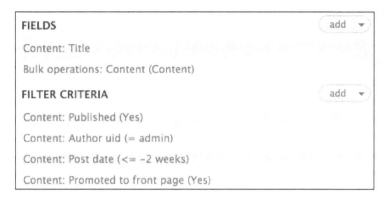

2. Go to **Configuration | Workflow | Rules | Components** and add a new **Action set** component. No parameters are needed; we will get the objects from the view.

3. Add a new Action, **Views Bulk Operations | Load a list of entity objects from a VBO View** and select the view we created in the first step, as shown in the following screenshot:

4. Optionally, enter a descriptive label for the variables and save the Action.

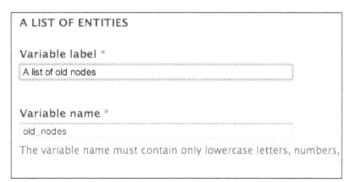

5. Add a new loop in the **Actions** section and select the VBO view result as the list data, shown as follows:

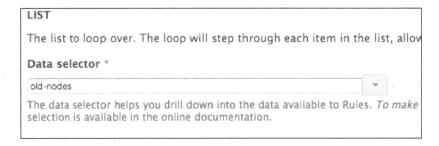

LIST

The list to loop over. The loop will step through each item in the list, allow

Data selector *

old-nodes

The data selector helps you drill down into the data available to Rules. *To make* selection is available in the online documentation.

6. Optionally, enter a descriptive label for the variable to be used in the loop.

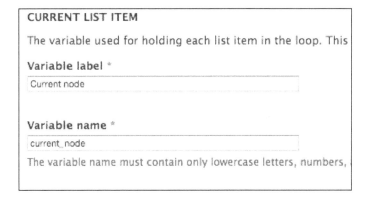

CURRENT LIST ITEM

The variable used for holding each list item in the loop. This

Variable label *

Current node

Variable name *

current_node

The variable name must contain only lowercase letters, numbers,

7. Add a new Action within the loop **Node | Remove content from front page**, as shown in the following screenshot:

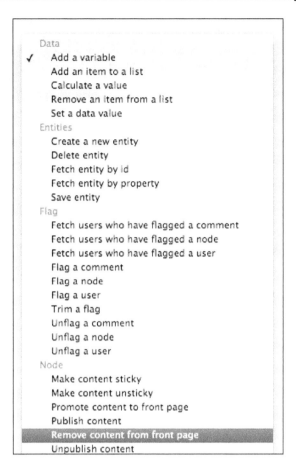

8. Select the current node to be removed from the front page.

How it works...

VBO views can be used to create a list of objects for Rules to execute an action on. This is a useful feature for developers and site builders who make extensive use of views on their sites. The advantage of using this feature is that we can create complex views with relationships and contextual filters (Rules provides an interface to pass arguments to views) and perform actions on the results.

In this example, we will create a new view that lists nodes that are created by user 1 (admin), are promoted to the front page, and are posted two weeks ago or earlier. Then, by adding a VBO field to the view, we make the results of the view available for Rules to use. Because the data type provided to Rules is a list, we can create a loop in our action and perform operations on each individual item.

Rules Bonus Pack (Should know)

This recipe describes some extra Rules functionality added by the **Rules Bonus Pack** module. This module is a set of extensions and integrations with other modules to extend Rules to provide additional Events, Conditions, and Actions and also integrate with other modules, such as CTools.

In this example, we will act on the node view by modifying the page title to include the node's associated taxonomy terms.

Getting ready

Download Rules Bonus Pack and enable **Rules Bonus: Miscellaneous**.

How to do it...

1. Create a new rule configuration, set the Event to **Node | Content is viewed**.

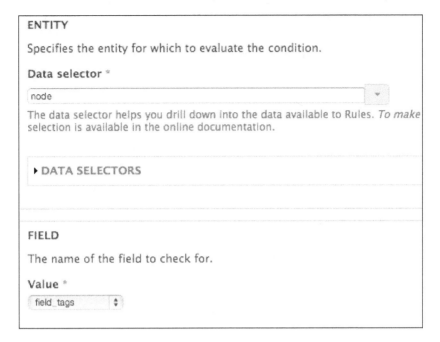

2. Add a Condition, **Entities | Entity has field**, use **node** as the entity and select **field_tags** as the field to check for.

3. Add an Action, **Rules Bonus: Miscellaneous | Set page title**.

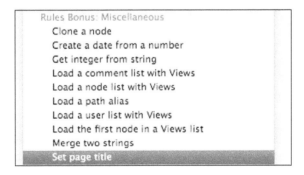

4. Use **REPLACEMENT PATTERNS** to modify the page title.

> TITLE TO SET
>
> Choose which page title should be set on this action.
>
> Value *
>
> [node:title] - [node:field-tags]

How it works...

In this example we've used a custom action provided by the Rules Bonus Pack module. We tell Rules to act on a node view by modifying the node's title, if it has any tags associated with it. For safety, we could also add a Condition, **Data | Data value is empty**, set it to **node:field-tags**, and check **Negate** to make sure we only do that if the node actually has terms.

There's more...

Rules Bonus Pack provides a number of essential extensions to the Rules framework. The following is a list of the main features:

▶   **CTools / Page manager integration**: Rules Bonus Pack provides a bridge between the Page manager and Rules. It can provide an Event for viewing each custom page variant, which is useful when using Panels and Rules together.

   Rules Bonus Pack also provides integration with the Page manager's Access control feature. We can create condition components that can be used by the Page manager to determine whether a user can access the custom page.

▶   **Blocks** and **Theme related Actions**: Rules Bonus Pack provides various Block and Theme related Actions. By enabling **Rules Bonus: Block** and **Rules Bonus: Theme** modules, we get access to various Actions, such as, placing a block in a region based on a condition or adding a custom CSS class to the body.

These recipes target developers who wish to extend Rules with their own custom Events, Conditions, and Actions. We'll also learn how to provide new entity tokens for Rules to use, how to execute rule configurations in code, and how to provide default rule configurations in our custom module.

The code snippets in these recipes are for demonstration purposes only. They are intended only to explain a specific hook or functionality and do not always provide a generic solution to a problem.

Providing new Events, Conditions, and Actions (Become an expert)

This recipe explains how to create our custom Events, Conditions, and Actions.

In this example, we'll act on a view that's being rendered on the site. We'll create a new condition, where we set the view that's being rendered, and in our action, we'll update a custom database table with the number of times the view has been rendered.

Getting ready

Enable the Views and Views UI modules, and create a view of the latest content on the site. In this example, we'll use the latest content as the view name, and create a block displaying the latest content by the admin that lists all new content posted by user 1.

We also need to create a new database table where we'll store the information; we'll call it `custom_view_render`. We use `hook_schema()` in our `.install` file so our custom table will be available in all supported database engines automatically.

How to do it...

1. Create a new custom module with the following structure:

```
{modules_folder}/custom/
  custom.info
  custom.module
  custom.rules.inc
  custom.install
```

2. Define the module's information in the `custom.info` file:

```
name = Custom
description = Provides an integration with the Rules framework to
store the number of times a view was rendered
core = 7.x
package = Rules Custom
dependencies[] = rules
dependencies[] = rules_admin
dependencies[] = views
dependencies[] = views_ui
```

3. Define our custom database table in the `custom.install` file:

```
/**
 * Implements hook_schema()
 */
function custom_schema() {
  $schema['custom_views_render'] = array (
    'description' => 'The base table for custom views render.',
    'fields' => array(
      'view' => array(
        'description' => 'The name and display ID of the view.',
        'type' => 'varchar',
        'length' => '32',
        'not null' => TRUE,
        'default' => '',
      ),
      'rendered' => array(
        'description' => 'The number of times the view was
rendered.',
        'type' => 'int',
        'unsigned' => TRUE,
        'not null' => TRUE,
      ),
    ),
    'primary key' => array('view'),
  );
  return $schema;
}
```

4. Define our new custom Event in `custom.rules.inc`:

```
/**
 * Implements hook_rules_event_info()
 * Define our new custom event for Rules
 */
function custom_rules_event_info() {
  return array(
    'custom_views_render' => array (
      'label' => 'A view is rendered',
      'group' => 'Rules Custom',
      'variables' => array(
        'view' => array(
          'type' => 'custom_view_datatype',
          'label' => t('View being rendered')
        )
      )
```

```
      )
    );
  }
```

5. Because views are not regular data types natively available to Rules; we provided the `custom_view_datatype` type as the variable type. We also need to define this new data type in our `hook_rules_data_info()` function:

```
/**
 * Implements hook_rules_data_info().
 * This hook should be used to define new data types to Rules.
 *
 * In this case, we simply pass on the view object to Rules
 */
function custom_rules_data_info() {
  return array(
    'custom_view_datatype' => array(
      'label' => t('view')
    ),
  );
}
```

6. We want Rules to invoke our event when a view is being rendered, so we'll use `hook_views_pre_render()` in custom.rules.inc and use `rules_invoke_event_by_args()` function to notify Rules that the event needs to be invoked:

```
/**
 * Implements hook_views_pre_render()
 * Invoke our custom event when a view is being rendered
 */
function custom_views_pre_render(&$view) {
  rules_invoke_event_by_args('custom_views_render', array($view));
}
```

7. Define our new Condition, that will compare a rendered view's name and display ID with a specified view:

```
/**
 * Implements hook_rules_condition_info()
 */
function custom_rules_condition_info() {
  return array(
    'custom_views_condition' => array(
      'label' => t('View being rendered'),
      'parameter' => array(
        'view' => array(
          'type' => 'text',
```

```
                    'label' => t('View and display'),
                    'options list' => 'custom_views_list',
                    'description' => t('Select the view and display ID'),
                    'restriction' => 'input',
                ),
            ),
            'group' => t('Rules Custom')
        )
    );
}
```

8. In the `options list` attribute, we define a custom function `custom_views_list` that returns an array of the available views on our site:

```
/**
 * Helper function that returns all available views on our site
 */
function custom_views_list() {
  $views = array();
  foreach (views_get_enabled_views() as $view_name => $view) {
    foreach ($view->display as $display_name => $display) {
      $views[$view_name . '-' . $display_name] =
      check_plain($view->human_name) . ' - ' . check_
plain($display->display_title);
    }
  }
  return $views;
}
```

9. The array key `custom_views_condition`, defined in our `custom_rules_condition_info()` function, will be used to execute the actual comparison that will return a Boolean value, so we'll add a function with the same name:

```
/**
 * Callback function for our custom condition
 * The function name must match the array key defined in hook_
rules_condition_info()
 */
function custom_views_condition($view = array()) {
  $current_view = views_get_current_view();
  $parts = explode('-', $view);
  if (($parts[0] == $current_view->name) && ($parts[1] ==
$current_view->current_display)) {
    return TRUE;
  }
  return FALSE;
}
```

10. Let's create our custom Action for Rules:

```
function custom_rules_action_info() {
  return array(
    'custom_update_table' => array(
      'label' => t('Update "custom_views_render" table'),
      'parameter' => array(
        'view' => array(
          'type' => 'custom_view_datatype',
          'label' => t('Rendered View'),
        ),
      ),
      'group' => t('Rules Custom')
    ),
  );
}
```

11. We also need to add a function that actually gets called by Rules when the action fires. The name of this function must match the value of the "base" attribute defined in `hook_rules_action_info()`:

```
/**
 * The database function that gets called by the Rules Action
 * The function name must match the value in the 'base' attribute
 * defined in hook_rules_action_info()
 */
function custom_update_table($view) {
    if (!is_object($view)) {
      return FALSE;
    }
    $result = db_select('custom_views_render', 'c')
      ->fields('c')
      ->condition('view', $view->name .'_'. $view->current_
display, '=')
      ->execute()
      ->fetchAssoc();

    if ($result) {
      $update = db_update('custom_views_render')
      ->expression('rendered', 'rendered + :one', array(':one' =>
1))
      ->condition('view', $view->name .'_'. $view->current_
display, '=')
      ->execute();
    }
    else {
```

```
        $insert = db_insert('custom_views_render')
        ->fields(array(
          'view' => $view->name .'_'. $view->current_display,
          'rendered' => 1
        ))
        ->execute();
      }
    }
```

The last step is to create a new rule configuration, set the Event to **Rules Custom | A view is rendered**, add a Condition **Rules Custom | View being rendered** and set it to our latest content view, and add an Action **Update "custom_views_render" table**:

12. Set the Event.

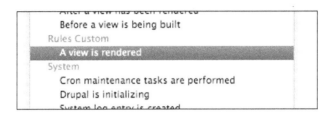

13. Add the Condition.

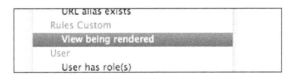

14. Set the view and display ID in the Condition, as shown in the following screenshot:

15. Add our custom Action:

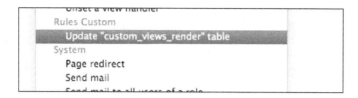

16. Set the rendered view's **Data selector** value to the view object provided by our event:

> RENDERED VIEW
>
> Data selector *
>
> | view | ▼ |
> | --- | --- |
>
> The data selector helps you drill down into the data available to Rules. *To* selection is available in the online documentation.

How it works...

In this example, we're creating a custom workflow by providing a new Event, Condition, and Action. In this virtual example, we want to track how many times a given view has been rendered. First we create a new database table to store the data in. Then we define our custom Event (**A view is rendered**) and our Condition (**View being rendered**) where we can choose the view and display that's being rendered. In the last step, we define our Action (**Update "custom_views_render" table**) which takes care of the database operations. Then we go ahead and create the rule configuration using our new Event, Condition, and Action.

It is the best practice to add all Rules hooks to a custom `*.rules.inc` file. Rules will automatically detect this file and fire the hooks.

There's more...

The following sections provide more information on creating Events, Conditions and Actions, and clearing caches.

Events

To create new Events for Rules, we need to implement `hook_rules_event_info()`. In this hook we need to return an array of Events, with the keys becoming the machine readable names of the Events. We can define the label, group, and variables this event will use. We can then fire this event by using `rules_invoke_event()` or `rules_invoke_event_by_args()` in another function or hook.

Conditions

We can define new Conditions by implementing `hook_rules_condition_info()`. Again, we need to return an array of Conditions with the array keys becoming the machine readable names of the Conditions, and by default, Rules will look for a function with the same name which will be fired when the Condition is invoked. Therefore, we need to create a function using the same machine readable name.

We must also define the parameters used by the condition. These parameters will be used in the custom function that returns either `TRUE` or `FALSE`.

Actions

When defining new Actions, we need to implement `hook_rules_action_info()`. Actions have a similar structure to Conditions, the definition consists of an array with information about the Action and a callback function that gets fired. The main difference is that an Action may execute an operation or return additional data for Rules.

Clearing the caches

Rules and the Entity API uses a fair amount of caching in order to increase performance. Therefore these caches need to be cleared every time a new Event, Condition, or Action is defined.

Providing new entity tokens (Become an expert)

This recipe demonstrates how to provide new entity tokens for Rules. **Entity tokens** provides a way to use placeholders in Rules (and other modules) and dynamically replace them with chunks of data.

In this example, we'll provide the current number of registered users on our site as a globally available token for Rules.

How to do it...

1. Implement `hook_entity_property_info()` to provide our new entity token:

```
/**
 * Implements hook_entity_property_info()
 * We extend the natively available 'site' properties
 */
function custom_entity_property_info() {
    $info = array();
    $properties = &$info['site']['properties'];
    $properties['registered_users'] = array(
```

```
      'label' => t("Number of registered users"),
      'type' => 'integer',
      'description' => t("Returns the current number of registered
users on the site."),
      'getter callback' => 'custom_number_of_users'
   );
   return $info;
}
```

2. We've defined `custom_number_of_users` as the callback function in the `getter callback` property, so we'll create this function:

```
/**
 * Callback function that returns the current number of registered
users
 */
function custom_number_of_users() {
   $result = db_query("SELECT count(*) FROM {users} WHERE uid >
1")->fetchField();
   return $result;
}
```

3. The newly created entity token will be available to use in Conditions and Actions in **REPLACEMENT PATTERNS**:

▼ REPLACEMENT PATTERNS	
Note that token replacements containing chained objects – replacement patterns. See the online documentation for m	
Replacement patterns for *Site information*	
TOKEN	LABEL
[site:name]	Name
[site:slogan]	Slogan
[site:mail]	Email
[site:url]	URL
[site:url-brief]	URL (brief)
[site:login-url]	Login page
[site:registered-users]	Number of registered users

How it works...

By implementing `hook_entity_property_info()`, we're providing the Entity API information about our new entity token. The function that returns data needs to be defined in the `getter callback` property. Implementing this hook makes it possible to use new tokens in the rule configurations, or any other configuration that uses Entity API.

Executing Rules programmatically (Become an expert)

This recipe explains how to execute Actions, Rules, or Rule sets programmatically.

In this example, we'll create a simple component that sends an e-mail to the site administrators and execute this component programmatically.

How to do it...

1. Add a new action set component, call it **Send message to all admins**:

2. Add a new Action, **System | Send message to all users of a role**.
3. Select administrators in the **ROLES** select box:

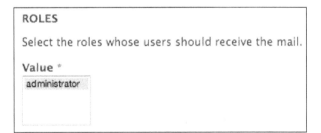

4. Enter some text to the **SUBJECT** text field:

> SUBJECT
>
> The mail's subject.
>
> **Value** *
>
> Hello Admin!

5. Enter a message and save the component:

> MESSAGE
>
> The mail's message body.
>
> **Value** *
>
> This is a message...

6. Now that we've created our component, we can execute it in our custom module using `rules_invoke_component()`:

```php
<?php
rules_invoke_component('send_message_to_all_admins');
?>
```

How it works...

Components can be executed programmatically using the `rules_invoke_component()` function. The first parameter of the function will receive the machine readable name of the component, followed by any additional parameters that the component requires. This way we can execute complex Actions, Rules, Rule sets, Conditions, or additional plugins defined by other modules.

The following section describes the execution of standalone plugins programmatically.

Executing standalone plugins

It's also possible to programmatically execute plugins without combining them into a component. We can, for example, execute a Condition in the following way:

```php
<?php
$condition = rules_condition('user_has_role', array('role' =>
array('editor')));
$condition->execute($user);
?>
```

Providing new variables for Actions (Become an expert)

This example explains how to modify existing or provide new variables and data for Rules in Actions.

We'll extend our previously defined action with a new one that provides additional data to Rules after the action is executed. In this case, the data provided to Rules is the number of currently registered users on the site.

Getting ready

This recipe is based on the recipe *Providing new Events, Conditions, and Actions* (*Become an expert*) in this book.

How to do it...

1. Add a new associative array to our `hook_rules_action_info()` function and instead of "parameters" we'll use the "provides" property:

```php
'custom_registered_users' => array(
'label' => t('Get number of registered users'),
    'provides' => array(
      'number_of_users' => array(
        'type' => 'integer',
        'label' => t('Number of users')
      ),
    ),
    'group' => t('Rules Custom')
)
```

2. Create the callback function that returns an array in the format Rules expects it:

```
/**
 * Callback function that returns the current number
 * of registered users and returns it to Rules in an
 * array
 */
  function custom_registered_users() {
     $result = db_query("SELECT count(*) FROM {users} WHERE uid >
1")
     ->fetchField();
     // Return an array for Rules with the array key
     // being the machine readable name defined in the
     // 'provides' property
     return array(
        'number_of_users' => $result
     );
  }
```

3. After clearing caches, the newly created action will be available in the list of Actions:

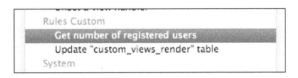

4. Optionally we can modify the variable's label and suggested machine readable name in the next configuration screen.

NUMBER OF USERS

Variable label *

Number of users

Variable name *

number_of_users

The variable name must contain only lowercase letters, numbers,

When adding additional Actions our new variable becomes available to Rules. For the purpose of this example, we'll add the Action, **System | Show a message on the site** and display the results in the **MESSAGE** field. Note that the created variable doesn't become available as a token, so we need to **Switch to data selection** and select the variable from the drop-down list.

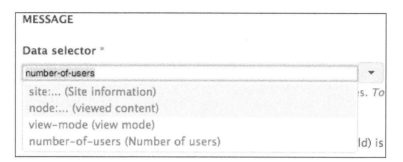

How it works...

Actions can provide new variables to Rules by making use of the `provides` property in `hook_rules_action_info()`. The data structure is almost identical to the way we declare parameters, the only difference is that user input is not allowed. By providing new variables to Rules, we can execute complex functions in an action and then work with their return data while still in Rules.

Providing default rule configurations (Become an expert)

This recipe explains how to provide default rule configurations in code. The advantage of that is that we can keep our configurations in code and use version control, such as, SVN or Git.

How to do it...

1. In our custom module's folder, we add a new file called `custom.rules_defaults.inc` and declare the rule configuration by implementing `hook_default_rules_configuration()`. The contents of the file are as follows:

    ```
    /**
     * Implements hook_default_rules_configuration()
     */
    function custom_default_rules_configuration() {
      $rule = rules_reaction_rule();
      $rule->label = 'Default Rule';
    ```

```
    $rule->active = TRUE;
    $rule->event('node_insert')
    ->condition('data_is', array('data:select' => 'node:type',
'value' => 'article'))
    ->condition(rules_condition('data_is', array('data:select' =>
'node:author:uid', 'value' => 1))->negate())
    ->action('drupal_message', array('message' => 'Hey
[node:author], thanks for creating a new article!'));

    $configs['custom_default_rule'] = $rule;
    return $configs;
}
```

2. After clearing the caches, our newly created default rule will become available in the list of configurations, as shown in the following screenshot:

Active rules

NAME

Default Rule

Machine name: custom_default_rule, Weight: 0

How it works...

Using `hook_default_rules_configuration()`, we can define our rule configuration in code using Rules' methods for Events, Conditions, and Actions. Rules will look for a file `*.rules_defatuls.inc` in our module's folder, and automatically add our default rule to the available configurations after clearing the caches.

There's more...

Rules is compatible with the `Features` module, which provides a centralized API for exporting and importing configuration from the database. This is also an effective way to manage configuration in code and version control systems.

Altering default rule configurations

It is also possible to modify a default rule configuration in code. For that we could use `hook_default_rules_configuration_alter()` in our `*.rules_defaults.inc` file.

```
/**
 * Implements hook_default_rules_configuration_alter()
 */
function custom_default_rules_configuration_alter(&$configs) {
    $configs['custom_default_rule']->condition('data_is',
array('data:select' => 'node:is_new', 'value' => TRUE));
}
```

Making changes to the configuration on the UI

Rules tracks the state of a Rule configuration that has been added programmatically. What that means is that it can determine whether an imported configuration is in its default state (not modified compared to the code) or overridden (modified using the UI, but not in code). When a configuration is modified, Rules allows to **revert** it back to its original state.

edit	translate	disable	clone	revert

By clicking on that, we're telling Rules that it should re-read the configuration that we've defined in code and revert it to its original state.

Thank you for buying
Drupal Rules How-to

About Packt Publishing

Packt, pronounced 'packed', published its first book "*Mastering phpMyAdmin for Effective MySQL Management*" in April 2004 and subsequently continued to specialize in publishing highly focused books on specific technologies and solutions.

Our books and publications share the experiences of your fellow IT professionals in adapting and customizing today's systems, applications, and frameworks. Our solution based books give you the knowledge and power to customize the software and technologies you're using to get the job done. Packt books are more specific and less general than the IT books you have seen in the past. Our unique business model allows us to bring you more focused information, giving you more of what you need to know, and less of what you don't.

Packt is a modern, yet unique publishing company, which focuses on producing quality, cutting-edge books for communities of developers, administrators, and newbies alike. For more information, please visit our website: www.packtpub.com.

About Packt Open Source

In 2010, Packt launched two new brands, Packt Open Source and Packt Enterprise, in order to continue its focus on specialization. This book is part of the Packt Open Source brand, home to books published on software built around Open Source licences, and offering information to anybody from advanced developers to budding web designers. The Open Source brand also runs Packt's Open Source Royalty Scheme, by which Packt gives a royalty to each Open Source project about whose software a book is sold.

Writing for Packt

We welcome all inquiries from people who are interested in authoring. Book proposals should be sent to author@packtpub.com. If your book idea is still at an early stage and you would like to discuss it first before writing a formal book proposal, contact us; one of our commissioning editors will get in touch with you.

We're not just looking for published authors; if you have strong technical skills but no writing experience, our experienced editors can help you develop a writing career, or simply get some additional reward for your expertise.

LiveCode Mobile Development Beginner's Guide

ISBN: 978-1-84969-248-9   Paperback: 246 pages

Create fun-filled, rich apps for Android and iOS with LiveCode

1. Create fun, interactive apps with rich media features of LiveCode

2. Step by step instructions for creating apps and interfaces

3. Dive headfirst into mobile application development using LiveCode backed with clear explanations enriched with ample screenshots

FreeCAD [How-to]

ISBN: 978-1-84951-886-4   Paperback: 70 pages

Solid Modeling with the power of python

1. Packed with simple and interesting examples of python coding for the CAD world.

2. Understand FreeCAD's approach to modeling and see how Python puts unprecedented power in the hands of users.

3. Dive into FreeCAD and its underlying scripting language.

Please check **www.PacktPub.com** for information on our titles

Intelligent Document Capture with Ephesoft

ISBN: 978-1-84969-372-1   Paperback: 182 pages

Learn to use open source software to automate the processing of scanned and digital documents to save time, save money, and improve accuracy

1. Learn the benefits of intelligent document capture and how to implement document capture using Ephesoft

2. Capture relevant information from your documents, even if they vary widely in format and appearance

3. Leverage the power of open source software to implement a cost effective solution for document capture

Drupal 7 Cookbook

ISBN: 978-1-84951-796-6   Paperback: 324 pages

Over 70 recipes that will advance your Drupal skills from novice to pro

1. Install, set up, and manage a Drupal site and discover how to get the most out of creating and displaying content

2. Become familiar with creating new content types and use them to create and publish content using Views, Blocks, and Panels

3. Learn how to work with images, documents, and video and how to integrate them with Facebook, Twitter, and Add this

Please check **www.PacktPub.com** for information on our titles

www.ingramcontent.com/pod-product-compliance
Lightning Source LLC
LaVergne TN
LVHW080104070326
832902LV00014B/2412